M000026834

UNITAS

Couple's Workbook

JOANN HEANEY-HUNTER, PH.D.
LOUIS H. PRIMAVERA, PH.D.

UNITAS
PREPARING FOR
SACRAMENTAL MARRIAGE

Couple's Workbook

A Herder & Herder Book

THE CROSSROAD PUBLISHING COMPANY • NEW YORK

The Crossroad Publishing Company
481 Eighth Avenue, New York, N.Y. 10001

Copyright © 1998 by Joann Heaney-Hunter, Ph.D. and Louis H. Primavera, Ph.D.

All rights reserved. No part of this book may be reproduced, stored in a retrieval system, or transmitted, in any form or by any means, electronic, mechanical, photocopying, recording, or otherwise, without the written permission of The Crossroad Publishing Company.

Nihil obstat: Rev. Msgr. John J. Strynkowski, S.T.D.
Censor delegatus
March 24th, 1998

Imprimatur: ✠ John R. McGann, D.D.
Bishop of Rockville Centre
April 3rd, 1998

Scripture quotations are from the New Revised Standard Version of the Bible, copyright © 1989 by the Division of Christian Education of the National Council of the Churches of Christ in the USA. Used by permission. All rights reserved.

Printed in the United States of America.

The following *Unitas* materials are now available
from The Crossroad Publishing Company:

Unitas Leader's Guide   ISBN: 0-8245-1755-5
Unitas Couple's Workbook   ISBN: 0-8245-1756-3
Unitas 1 set videotapes   ISBN: 0-8245-1757-1

Unitas Couple's Workbook   0-8245-1756-3

To our life partners and best friends,

Greg and Anne,

who have helped us to understand

the true meaning of marriage in love and faith.

ℒ

Contents

Acknowledgments

Unitas would not have been possible without the help of many people. We thank the following for their time, talent, and financial support.

Special thanks to the following members of FADICA (Foundations and Donors Interested in Catholic Activities) for generously funding the development of *Unitas*: St. Marys Catholic Foundation; RASKOB Foundation; Frank J. Lewis Foundation; Trust Funds Incorporated; Komes Foundation; and one anonymous donor. We also thank Francis Butler, President of FADICA, for his invaluable advice and expertise.

We have found support and assitance from many members of the St. John's University community. Without their willingness to support the research and development of *Unitas*, this work would never have been possible. Thanks go to: Rev. Gerard Ettlinger and Rev. Jean-Pierre Ruiz, Chairs of the Department of Theology and Religious Studies; Dr. Willard Gingerich, Dean of the Graduate School of Arts and Sciences; Mr. Victor Ramos and the staff of the Office of Grants and Research; Ms. Leslie Bogen and Ms. Alicia DiBenedetto, graduate assistants for the project; staff members of the Offices of Printing and Reproduction Services; staff members of the Office of Travel Services; and Mrs. Lois Horan, for her assistance with the *Unitas* Conference.

The advisory board provided expert critique and support, especially during the early stages of this project. We gratefully acknowledge the assistance of Bishop Edmond Carmody, Diocese of Tyler, Texas; Dr. H. Richard McCord, Executive Director of the NCCB Secretariat for Marriage, Family, Laity, Women and Youth; Sr. Barbara Markey, Director of the Office of Family Ministry, Archdiocese of Omaha; and Rev. Gerard Ringenback, Pastor of St. Peter the Apostle Church, Islip Terrace, New York.

Two parishes, St. Peter the Apostle in Islip Terrace and Our Lady of Nazareth in Roanoke, Virginia, worked with us in the development stage of *Unitas*. The quality of this process was greatly enhanced by their wisdom, patience and energy. Special thanks go to Fr. Gerard Ringenback, Peggy and Richard Nixdorf, and the entire marriage formation team of St. Peter the Apostle Church, and to Fr. Joseph Lehmann, Roberta Small, Fr. Kenneth Stofft, and the entire marriage formation team of Our Lady of Nazareth Church. In a special way, we thank Roberta Small for her work on several *Unitas* rituals, and Dan and Lynn Lonnquist for their work on the inquiry session. We have been blessed by the gifts of these wonderful people and will always treasure their friendship as well as their contributions to *Unitas*.

During the course of testing, we have had the privilege of working with outstanding people all across the United States. Marriage preparation teams from the parishes listed below assisted in testing *Unitas* rituals and sessions. In addition, we wish to thank the following parish and diocesan leaders: Mr. and Mrs. Butch and Linda Moses, Holy Family of Nazareth, Irving, Texas; Fr. Lowell Case, Our Lady of Perpetual Help, Washington, D.C.; Msgr. Joseph Bynon, Resurrection Ascencion, Rego Park, New York; Deacon James Healy and Fr. Brendan O'Sullivan, St. Anthony, Sacramento California; Fr. Joseph Genito, O.S.A., St. Augustine, Casselbury, Florida; Ms. Diana Gaillardetz, St. Cecelia, Houston, Texas; Fr. Mike Vetrano, St. Elizabeth, Melville, New York; Fr. Mel Hemann, St. Joseph, Rickardsville, Iowa; Deacon Ralph Imholte, St. Mary's, Colt's Neck, New Jersey; Fr. Roy Tvrdik, St. Mary Gate of Heaven, Ozone Park, New York; Fr. Phil Pryzbyla, St. Patrick's, Canonsburg, Pennsylvania; Fr. John McGratty, Sts. Peter and Paul, Manorville, New York; Mr. and Mrs. Wally and Winnie Honeywell, St. Pius, Houston, Texas; and Ms. Josie Curtis, Diocese of Beaumont, Texas.

The leadership of the Diocese of Rockville Centre, New York, has encouraged and supported the development of *Unitas*. Special thanks to Bishop John McGann for his continuing commitment to marriage and family, and Msgr. Frank Schneider, Chancellor, for his willingness to make marriage and family issues a priority in the diocese. You will always have a special place in our minds and hearts. We are grateful to Sr. Lauren Hanley of the Office of Pastoral Formation for working with us on the important task of marriage preparation training. Her insights and expertise contributed greatly to the development of our training efforts, and her friendship has been a source of constant support. We also thank Mr. Mike O'Leary, Ms. Rose Russo, and the staff at TeLIcare for their efforts in the development of the videotapes.

We gratefully acknowledge the efforts of Msgr. John Strynkowski of the Diocese of Brooklyn for his careful reading of *Unitas*. Thanks also to Fr. John Costello, Director of Family Ministry for the Diocese of Brooklyn, for his support and willingness to make *Unitas* known throughout the diocese.

We received expert post-production advice and assistance on the videotapes from Doug Fisher of Fisher Productions. His knowledge of theology and pastoral issues has helped us tremendously.

We thank Crossroad Publishing for their belief in *Unitas* and for their willingness to bring to publication this complex project. Our deepest gratitude goes to Lynn Schmitt Quinn, our editor throughout the project. She has been coach, cheerleader, unfailing professional, and good friend. She is any author's vision of what an editor should be. Without her careful eye, attention to detail, and willingness to work, *Unitas* would never have been completed.

In a special way, we would like to thank our parents, Joan and Tom Heaney, and Julie and Bert Primavera. Over the years, they have been our first teachers of love and faith. We thank them for the gift of life, and the gift of example that they have been for us.

Finally, our families are the source of *Unitas*. From them we have learned about who we are, about marriage, and about life. They have helped us to grow, to love, and to live. They have enabled us to reach far beyond ourselves. Each day, they actualize the phrase from *Les Miserables*, "To love another person is to see the face of God." We thank you, Greg, Beth and Kate, and Anne, Jim, Bill and Felissa, for helping *us* to see the face of God.

Welcome!

Dear Engaged Couple,

Congratulations on your upcoming marriage, and welcome to *Unitas*! We hope that by participating in *Unitas* you gain insights about your relationship with each other and with the Church community.

Unitas is a step beyond most "pre-Cana" and other marriage preparation programs. It is a sacramental formation process, designed to help you recognize that you are an important part of the Church community, and to help you build skills for a faith-filled married life.

Although we do not believe that *Unitas* will answer all your questions—*that* will take a lifetime!—we do hope it will raise issues for you, such as: How do you build faith in your family? How do you foster good communication? How do you develop a mature Christian conscience? How do you grow in intimacy? How do you resolve some practical issues that may affect you as a family? We hope that you will think about the things we share with you, and draw on them at various times in your lives.

We have designed *Unitas* so that each session is about two to two-and-one-half hours of content, discussion, and activities. Each session begins and ends with a brief prayer or Bible reading. Many of the readings we have selected are appropriate for weddings. The weekly activities are designed to reinforce the central elements of each session. They are important because they give you the opportunity to reflect on the session after it is over. Please take the time to complete the activities—the more you put into them, the more you will get out of them! At the beginning of each session, the married couples will ask if you have any questions or insights about the activities. If you would like to share your insights with the group, please feel free to do so.

Unitas also includes an opportunity for you to evaluate the presentations and activities. The evaluations are a critical part of the process, because they will help parish communities make *Unitas* stronger in the future. Please complete the forms and return them to the married leaders for their review. Your input is greatly appreciated and needed.

Thank you for being a part of *Unitas*. We hope it helps you now and in the future. We wish you the very best in your marriage and hope you continue to grow in love and faith throughout your life together.

Cordially,

Joann Heaney-Hunter and Louis H. Primavera

Introduction to Unitas

"**P**reparation of young people for marriage and family life is more necessary than ever in our times." These words of Pope John Paul II, taken from his 1981 encyclical *Familiaris Consortio,* present us with a challenge. How do church communities give you the very best in marriage preparation? Pope John Paul states that the best marriage preparation should be "a journey of faith." We think that this journey includes developing skills for married life, learning about the Church's vision for marriage, and taking advantage of opportunities to participate in your local church community.

These are the starting points for *Unitas. Unitas* is a marriage preparation process that contains several special elements:

1. *Faith formation*—we think that integrating faith in our lives is an essential ingredient for the journey toward Christian marriage.

2. *Information* about topics that concern engaged couples today.

3. *Opportunities* for building connections with the local Church.

We think that *Unitas* provides a unique way of addressing the issues of Christian marriage in the midst of your local church community.

In many dioceses you will begin formal marriage preparation before you come to any session of *Unitas.* At the first meeting with your pastor or other marriage preparation leader, you may be asked to complete a couple inventory such as FOCCUS. This detailed questionnaire will help point out your areas of similarity and difference, and may highlight potential problems in your relationship. FOCCUS is an important tool, because it helps you figure out the issues that you may face in your marriage.

Whether or not you complete an inventory such as FOCCUS, your parish has decided that *Unitas* will be at the center of your time of preparation. What should you expect from it? First of all, remember that high quality marriage preparation such as *Unitas* takes time. *Unitas* includes seven content sessions, and at least three celebrations with your parish community. Some parishes will offer additional events such as a wedding liturgy planning session, an evening of reflection for engaged couples and their sponsors, and a Natural Family Planning workshop. Taking advantage of these events will enhance your time of preparation.

You will notice that *Unitas* includes several celebrations that connect you with your parish community. First, there are three occasions during the process when you will participate in rituals at Sunday Eucharist (Mass). At Mass, you will be asked to come before the community (usually to the front of the Church), and the priest will ask the community to pray for you and your marriage. Often the community will congratulate you by applauding for you after the prayer! You will then take your seats again, and Mass will continue. We include presentations at Sunday Eucharist because we believe that marriage is not just a private event, but a cause of celebration for the entire church. If you are not Catholic, we are not trying to get you to change religions. We simply want you to share in your fiancé's Catholic tradition as fully as possible, and share in the joy that your fiancé's community feels because you have decided to marry in the Catholic Church.

Second, as a part of *Unitas,* you will spend some time with a sponsor (or mentor) couple from the parish. Sponsors are couples who have volunteered to participate in *Unitas* with you. They may come to the sessions with you; they will pray with you at parish celebrations; they will be available to help you and to answer your questions.

Third, you will discover that many people in the parish are praying for you as you prepare for marriage. We think this is vital, because prayer is a powerful way to connect people and to help them draw closer to God. We hope you gain strength from the knowledge that many people think enough of you to pray for you and your marriage.

Many engaged couples do not realize this, but you are very important to our Church. You are concrete reminders of God's love in our midst, and represent to many people a willingness to make a commitment and a leap of faith with a person that you love. Your love and your witness are precious to the entire Church!

In the seven sessions of *Unitas,* you will share many things, including information and experience. *Unitas* is structured so that you will begin by exploring the Catholic Church's theology of marriage. This may sound very theoretical, but it is actually based on your experiences and hopes for marriage. In the second session, you will work on developing communication and negotiation strategies. This session is a crucial foundation piece, because once you've developed clear communication and negotiation strategies, you will be able to apply them to the other topics of *Unitas*.

The third session focuses on you as a person and on the family from which you have come. Understanding yourselves as people and being aware of how your background can affect your adult lives is an important component as you come to relationship. The more you understand yourselves and your attitudes toward life, the more open you may be to the possibility of growth and change in your lives and in your relationships. In session four, you move from a discussion of personality and family to a conversation about your values. You will be asking each other to share about your values and the way you make decisions. Session four offers a strategy for developing a mature conscience, so that you can have a better sense of how to make value judgments.

In session five, you will explore intimacy and sexuality. We believe that intimacy is at the heart of every relationship, and that sexuality is at the heart of who we are as people. The two, therefore, go hand in hand. Your sexual relationship is an important part of your marriage. The session on intimacy and sexuality is not, however, an explanation of sexual mechanics. Instead, it is a discussion about sexual communication, sexual attitudes, and sexual values.

Session six moves the discussion to the nuts and bolts of contemporary married life. In particular, you will focus on some of the stresses of married life today—especially the two-career or two-job household. How you balance your work and family life is very important today, and should result in some interesting discussions!

The final session brings us back full circle. We began *Unitas* with the theology of marriage, and we end with an experience of the spirituality of marriage. What does it mean to say that you "live spirituality" every day? How is spirituality integrated into all you do as married people? How do you understand the role of spirituality in your lives and how do you think you will build it in your new homes? These are questions that we hope you will address in the last session.

What is the format of *Unitas*? As we were developing the process, we felt that it should reflect a variety of styles. You will notice that there are different kinds of activities and approaches to each topic. Throughout the sessions, you will find discussion questions for couples, discussion questions for small and large groups, various questionnaires and checklists, opportunities for role playing, and other activities. We know that different people respond well to different activities—so we tried to vary them throughout the sessions.

You'll also notice that we begin and end every session with a prayer or a Bible reading. This serves a couple of purposes. First, we believe that *Unitas* should take place in the context of faith. Praying together is a wonderful way to express the idea that you are entering the journey of faith toward marriage. Second, in choosing Bible readings for *Unitas*, we were careful to include selections that you could use at your wedding celebration. While you should check with your priest or deacon about the exact wording of any reading, the selections from *Unitas* might give you some ideas about your wedding celebration.

We think *Unitas* will give you a unique opportunity to participate in high quality marriage formation in your local parish community. We hope that it helps you achieve a "deeper knowledge of the mystery of Christ and the Church, and the meaning of the grace and responsibility of Christian marriage" (Pope John Paul II, *Familiaris Consortio*, art. 66).

Prayer for the Week

The days are surely coming, says the Lord, when I will make a new covenant with the house of Israel and the house of Judah. It will not be like the covenant that I made with their ancestors when I took them by the hand to bring them out of the land of Egypt—a covenant that they broke, though I was their husband, says the Lord. But this is the covenant that I will make with the house of Israel after those days, says the Lord: I will put my law within them, and I will write it on their hearts; and I will be their God, and they shall be my people. No longer shall they teach one another, or say to each other, "Know the Lord," for they shall all know me, from the least of them to the greatest, says the Lord; for I will forgive their iniquity, and remember their sin no more.

JEREMIAH 31: 31-34

SESSION 1

Theology of Marriage

Session 1 has three purposes: (1) to welcome you to your parish community, (2) to introduce you to other engaged participants and (3) to explain what Catholic Christians believe about marriage. In many ways, Session 1 is the most difficult session, because everything is new, and you are not sure what is going to happen. We hope that this session will help reduce any anxiety you have about *Unitas*.

In Session 1 we hope to help you understand the Church's theology of marriage. In reflecting on this, it is best to start with your experience. What do you hope for in marriage? As we've worked with many couples across the country, we have heard about their hopes and dreams for marriage. Many couples hope, for example, that their marriage will be a commitment for life. They hope for love and trust in each other, and they hope for fidelity. Many couples that we have talked to also express the hope that someday they will have children.

> *Catholic Christians believe that marriage is an intimate partnership of life and love.*

What you may not know is that these hopes correspond, in many ways, to our theology of marriage. For example, Catholic Christians believe that marriage is an intimate partnership of life and love. (*Pastoral Constitution on the Church in the Modern World,* no. 48.) We also believe that marriage was created by God to be a permanent union of man and woman. It forms, therefore, an unbreakable bond. Finally, the Church asserts that openness to life is one of the hallmarks of the Christian marriage. So you can see, the hopes and dreams of many young couples are very similar to our Church's understanding of marriage!

> *Marriage was created by God to be a permanent union of man and woman, . . . an unbreakable bond.*

As a Church community, we also believe that marriage is a symbol, a concrete expression of your lives, your experiences, and your hopes. A good symbol actually makes present an important person or event. For example, a pressed red rose in your wallet may make many things present. It may signify an event—a date, an anniversary, or a special occasion. It may bring to mind a turning point in your relationship—you got engaged, or you made up after an argument. It may simply be a concrete reminder of the love you share as a couple. In any event, the rose is not just a dead flower that you have saved for no good reason. It makes present someone or something very significant. If it did not, you wouldn't be carrying it!

We believe that symbols are important in our lives. They help us to remember events and people, and they help to make them present to us in a concrete way.

As a Church, we believe that you are the most powerful symbols of marriage because you make real the ideals of faithfulness and partnership. We think that your relationship is so special that it not only shows human love, but points to God's unconditional love for us as well.

> *God has made a covenant with us— a sacred promise of faithfulness that will never be broken.*
>
> ℘

In Judeo-Christian tradition, we call this unconditional love a "covenant." We believe that God has made a covenant with us—a sacred promise of faithfulness that will never be broken. While many of you may know a great deal about contracts, you may not be so familiar with the notion of covenant. For example, in a contract, we express rights and obligations. If obligations are not met, we have legal remedies and recourse. In a covenant, we go beyond obligations to express unconditional love. A covenant calls people to be interrelated in love. Jewish people believe that God's covenant with us was expressed well by prophets such as Jeremiah: "I will be your God and you will be my people." Christians believe that God's covenant was fulfilled in Jesus Christ. We, as the Church, carry out the work of Jesus Christ today.

As Catholics, we believe that marriage is a good example of a covenant. In marriage, we pledge to share ourselves with our partner 100%. There is no room in a Christian marriage to say: "I gave my 50%, now you give yours, or else." In a legal contract, if I do not complete my part of a bargain, I can be sued for "breach of contract." In a covenant relationship, we try to give 100%, confident that our spouse will do the same. In the times when we can't give 100%, we believe that our spouses will help see us through. This may sound like a difficult challenge, but we believe that we can commit to a covenant relationship because God, through Jesus, is always with us. In short, the idea of covenant is central for our theology of marriage.

Marriage as a covenant is closely linked to marriage as a sacrament. A sacrament is a concrete expression of God's covenant with us. In marriage, *you* are the primary sacrament or symbol of God's covenant. Through your lives, you embody the unconditional love of God. In a sacramental marriage, you make Christ present in the Church and the world. The "sacrament of marriage" doesn't automatically happen on the wedding day—you will grow and develop as the "sacrament of marriage" every day of your lives. In sacramental marriage, you are the tangible symbol—not only of your love for each other, but of your love for God, and your witness to the entire Christian community.

We have a few final thoughts about this session. We know that for a number of reasons, some of you may feel uncomfortable about participating in Church-sponsored marriage formation. For example, some of you may have been separated from the Church for a period of time. We hope that you will find us to be a community full of faith in Jesus Christ and concern for each other. Some of you are not Catholic, but are coming to marriage formation in the Catholic Church. We assure you that we respect you and your religious traditions. Furthermore, we guarantee that we will not try to convert you. What we will try to do is acquaint you with our traditions and beliefs about the sacredness of marriage. We also will try to help you understand what we expect of your Catholic fiancé who marries in the Church.

Some of you may not like group processes. We hope to make this as comfortable for you as possible. However, you will be discussing important subjects, which are sometimes threatening. Sticking with the process will help you to get to the heart of issues that are vital to the success of your future marriage. Whatever the reasons for your discomfort, we hope you will come to appreciate the value of *Unitas*, and that you will be more comfortable at the end of the process than you were at the beginning.

Sacramental marriage is not simply a private event in the lives of two people; it is a transforming event for the entire Christian community. We all share in the joy when two people declare that they will be witnesses of Christ through their life together.

In marriage, you are the primary sacrament or symbol of God's covenant.

Sacramental marriage is not simply a private event in the lives of two people; it is a transforming event for the entire Christian community.

ACTIVITY FOR THE WEEK

Couple Discussion on Symbols

· HIS SHEET ·

The activity for Session 1 is designed to help you reflect on the meaning of the symbols in your relationship, and the importance of "covenant" in your marriage. Take some time this week to think about these questions, and answer them using the following procedure.

- First, sit by yourselves and write out answers to the following questions on your individual worksheets. Use the other side if you need more space.
- Next, exchange your answers and read them by yourselves.
- Discuss your answers, pointing out areas of agreement and trying to resolve any disagreements.
- Try to write a joint answer to the following questions.

Discussion Questions

1. What are some of the most important symbols in our relationship?

2. How have we experienced the meaning of "covenant" in our relationship?

1. What are some of the most important symbols in our relationship?

2. How have we experienced the meaning of "covenant" in our relationship?

ACTIVITY FOR THE WEEK

Couple Discussion on Symbols

· HER SHEET ·

 The activity for Session 1 is designed to help you reflect on the meaning of the symbols in your relationship, and the importance of "covenant" in your marriage. Take some time this week to think about these questions, and answer them using the following procedure.

- First, sit by yourselves and write out answers to the following questions on your individual worksheets. Use the other side if you need more space.
- Next, exchange your answers and read them by yourselves.
- Discuss your answers, pointing out areas of agreement and trying to resolve any disagreements.
- Try to write a joint answer to the following questions.

Discussion Questions

1. What are some of the most important symbols in our relationship?

2. How have we experienced the meaning of "covenant" in our relationship?

Her Discussion Worksheet

1. What are some of the most important symbols in our relationship?

2. How have we experienced the meaning of "covenant" in our relationship?

Prayer for the Week

If I speak in the tongues of mortals and of angels, but do not have love, I am a noisy gong or a clanging cymbal. And if I have prophetic powers, and understand all mysteries and all knowledge, and if I have all faith, so as to remove mountains, but do not have love, I am nothing. If I give away all my possessions, and if I hand over my body so that I may boast, but do not have love, I gain nothing.

Love is patient; love is kind; love is not envious or boastful or arrogant or rude. It does not insist on its own way; it is not irritable or resentful; it does not rejoice in wrongdoing but rejoices in the truth. It bears all things, believes all things, hopes all things, endures all things. Love never ends.

And now faith, hope and love abide, these three; and the greatest of these is love.

I Corinthians 13: 1-7, 13

SESSION 2

Communication Skills

Session 2 has two purposes: (1) to introduce some key principles of effective communication and (2) to develop skills for successful communication through negotiation.

Most experts in marriage and family agree that effective communication is absolutely vital to any relationship. Like so many other areas of marriage, we think that communication is a *process* that develops over the life of the marriage. This means that even if you communicate very well, there is always room for growth and improvement. Enhancing your communication skills will take place throughout *Unitas* and beyond it. We hope that you will continue to develop your communication skills throughout your life together.

> *Communication is a process that develops over the life of the marriage.*
>
>

One of the things that we have come to believe is that marital communication can be risky—because the more you know about each other, the more you can hurt each other. Think about a time when you have shared a deep secret with your partner. What was his or her reaction? Did he or she accept you? Were you afraid that he or she would not? It is only possible to risk communicating openly because you trust and respect each other. These qualities grow as healthy relationships grow. For example, when you first met your fiancé, was it hard to trust him or her? As the relationship grew, did your trust and respect for that person grow as well? Trust and respect enable us to engage in the risky business of sharing our lives with each other.

The Church community emphasizes that every person has the right to be treated with respect in marriage. Marriage can never be an excuse for abusing your spouse. While some people think that abuse is primarily physical or sexual, it is also possible to abuse a person by failing to communicate with love and respect. For example, constant put-downs can be a sign of difficulties in communication. Remember that abuse need not be physical or sexual to cause permanent damage. Effective, loving marital communication requires that we not abuse each

"The unity of marriage, distinctly recognized by our Lord, is made clear in the equal personal dignity which must be accorded to husband and wife in mutual and unreserved affection."
—GAUDIUM ET SPES, NO. 49

✍

other with our words or the meanings behind our words.

We as a Church also affirm that good marriages require equality. While this does not mean that every person fulfills the same roles in every marriage, it does mean that partners respect each other's equal dignity. The Second Vatican Council states that "the unity of marriage, distinctly recognized by our Lord, is made clear in the equal personal dignity which must be accorded to husband and wife in mutual and unreserved affection." (See *Gaudium et Spes*, no. 49). Equal dignity means that you can communicate freely with each other, share in decision-making, and consider yourselves to be equal partners in the relationship. Regardless of what roles you have in your marriage—you are equal partners.

Communicating successfully includes a variety of skills. You must be able to share your thoughts and feelings with your partner. Good communication depends upon the ability to express yourself well. All of us can work on clearly articulating our thoughts and feelings to each other. One way that you can work on expressing yourself clearly is by saying what you mean and meaning what you say. It may be difficult to admit it or to even realize it, but the fact remains—all of us, at times, send mixed messages. Have you ever said to someone: "I feel fine," but your tone of voice or facial expression indicated that you were not fine? What you may want is for someone to probe more deeply into your feelings, or to ask again about them. If your partner does not pick up on the mixed message, you may wind up feeling hurt and upset. It is much more effective to say what you mean so your partner can get the message easily!

Forgiveness is an integral part of communication.

✍

Effective communication also involves learning to listen well. Listening is more than hearing sounds, it is attending to what your partner says and means. Listening for the meaning behind the words is very important in marital communication. Think about our discussion of symbols in the last session. Our communication is symbolic also, because there can be many layers of meaning behind the words or gestures we use. Good listening takes energy, because it involves paying attention to what your partner is saying or doing, and responding appropriately. It also involves paying attention to your partner's non-verbal signals, and understanding the messages behind them.

All relationships become stronger and healthier as we work through our conflicts in a spirit of forgiveness and reconciliation.

✍

We also believe that forgiveness is an integral part of communication. Everyone must learn to forgive and be forgiven when conflict arises, as it inevitably will. All relationships become stronger and healthier as we work through our conflicts in a spirit of forgiveness and reconciliation. It is very hard to admit that we are all fallible—but we are. Forgiving each other and being forgiven can be a very powerful form of communication in your relationship.

Furthermore, in any marriage that is built on faith, shared prayer can grow and develop as communication develops. Developing a shared prayer life takes many years and much effort! Many couples do not pray together, nor do they feel comfortable praying together. In Christian marriage, however, communicating in faith through prayer is an important part of life.

Shared prayer can grow and develop as communication develops.

We know that some of you come from a variety of religious traditions, even though you are preparing for marriage in the Catholic Church. For you, shared prayer can be a way to enhance communication about faith. Talk about the ways you can pray in common, about the traditions that you share. Think of the ways you can communicate about the similarities and the differences in your faith traditions. For example, Christians and Jews share the belief that the books of the Hebrew Scriptures are sacred. If you are a Catholic–Jewish couple, try praying together with the psalms. Try reflecting on the prophet Isaiah or the creation accounts in the book of Genesis. There are many elements of faith that you share—talk about them, and pray about them together

Conflict in a marriage is not necessarily a problem— resolving conflict is part of life.

It is important to recognize that communication in marriage frequently involves negotiation. Conflict in a marriage is not necessarily a problem—resolving conflict is part of life. For example, in marriage, we have certain responsibilities to fulfill for and with each other. Failure to fulfill them will cause conflict in the relationship. We also come to the relationship with expectations and agendas—some realistic and some unrealistic. We enter into marriage assuming that these expectations will be met. Unmet expectations can cause conflict in marriage relationships.

Negotiation seeks to resolve conflict in a way that satisfies both parties. In successful negotiation, agendas are identified, expectations met, responsibilities fulfilled, and needs and wants satisfied. Negotiation involves a process of dialogue about an issue, an idea, or a concrete thing. Through negotiation, we usually get something that we want, but we also give up or let go of something in order to achieve the goal. In other words, successful negotiation

Negotiation seeks to resolve conflict in a way that satisfies both parties.

Successful negotiation creates a win-win situation through a process of giving up and letting go.

∽

creates a win-win situation through a process of giving up and letting go. Following the steps for negotiation should help provide a framework for better conflict resolution in your marriage.

Effective communication in marriage is one concrete way that you can witness to the love of Christ in your lives. When you communicate effectively, you have the opportunity to teach, by your example, the kindness, the care, and the love of Christ.

IN-SESSION ACTIVITIES

Communication Priorities Discussion

· HIS SHEET ·

Each person should take approximately five minutes to complete the following checklist. After you complete the list, exchange answers with your fiancée. Do you agree or disagree on these issues? Why or why not? Discuss your communication priorities with each other for seven to ten minutes.

Directions: The following is a list of elements that characterize communication. For each element, rate how important you believe each is in your communication with your future spouse.

Element	Extremely Important	Very Important	Moderately Important	Somewhat Important	Not Important
Partners treat each other as equals.					
Partners are willing to listen to each other.					
Partners try to be as honest as possible.					
Partners trust each other.					
Partners respect each other.					
Partners don't let their emotions interfere with their communication.					
Partners avoid asking questions that can't be answered.					
Partners make time to communicate.					

· 23 ·

Non-Verbal Communication Worksheet

· HIS SHEET ·

Please separate and write down all the non-verbal signals your partner uses when she is angry. After about five minutes, come together. Try to describe your own non-verbal signals to your partner. Do you agree about what you see? Maybe you need to be more aware of your non-verbal signals!

Communication Priorities Discussion

· HER SHEET ·

Each person should take approximately five minutes to complete the following checklist. After you complete the list, exchange answers with your fiancé. Do you agree or disagree on these issues? Why or why not? Discuss your communication priorities with each other for seven to ten minutes.

Directions: The following is a list of elements that characterize communication. For each element, rate how important you believe each is in your communication with your future spouse.

Element	Extremely Important	Very Important	Moderately Important	Somewhat Important	Not Important
Partners treat each other as equals.					
Partners are willing to listen to each other.					
Partners try to be as honest as possible.					
Partners trust each other..					
Partners respect each other.					
Partners don't let their emotions interfere with their communication.					
Partners avoid asking questions that can't be answered.					
Partners make time to communicate.					

℘

Non-Verbal Communication Worksheet

· HER SHEET ·

℘ Please separate and write down all the non-verbal signals your partner uses when he is angry. After about five minutes, come together. Try to describe your own non-verbal signals to your partner. Do you agree about what you see? Maybe you need to be more aware of your non-verbal signals!

ACTIVITY FOR THE WEEK

Couple Negotiation

· COUPLE SHEET ·

The purpose of this activity is to help you practice your negotiation skills. By completing this exercise some time during the week, we hope you will reinforce the most important points of the session on communication. If you feel that you cannot negotiate effectively, keep trying! It gets easier with practice.

Six Steps for Effective Negotiation

1. Clearly define the issues to be negotiated and write them down.

2. List points of agreement and disagreement.

3. Describe alternative courses of action.

4. Consider the possible positive and negative outcomes for each alternative.

5. Together, decide the most acceptable alternative.

6. **Together, make a plan to implement the chosen decision.**

Directions:
Some time this week, sit down with your partner to discuss an important issue. Agree to negotiate the solution. Use the steps above and the following worksheets to resolve the situation. Remember, successful negotiation creates a win-win situation because both parties are willing to give.

Couple Negotiation Worksheet

Step 1:   Write out the issue or problem to be negotiated.

Step 2:   List points of agreement and disagreement.

        A. Points of Agreement:

        B. Points of Disagreement:

Step 3:   Describe the alternative courses of action.

Step 4:   For each alternative course of action, list the positive and negative outcomes.

Step 5:   Decide the most acceptable course of action.

Step 6:   Make a plan to implement the chosen decision.

His Negotiation Worksheet

Step 1:   Write out the issue or problem to be negotiated.

Step 2:   List points of agreement and disagreement.

     A. Points of Agreement:

     B. Points of Disagreement:

Step 3:   Describe the alternative courses of action on the back of this page.

Step 4:   For each alternative course of action, list the positive and negative outcomes on the back of this page.

Step 5:   Decide the most acceptable course of action.

Step 6:   Make a plan to implement the chosen decision.

Step 3: Possible Courses of Action Worksheet

Step 4: Consequences Worksheet

Positive Outcomes	Negative Outcomes

Her Negotiation Worksheet

.Step 1:   Write out the issue or problem to be negotiated.

Step 2:   List points of agreement and disagreement.

    A. Points of Agreement:

    B. Points of Disagreement:

Step 3:   Describe the alternative courses of action on the back of this page.

Step 4:   For each alternative course of action, list the positive and negative outcomes on the back of this page.

Step 5:   Decide the most acceptable course of action.

Step 6:   Make a plan to implement the chosen decision.

Step 3: Possible Courses of Action Worksheet

Step 4: Consequences Worksheet

Positive Outcomes	Negative Outcomes

Prayer for the Week

O Lord, you have searched me and known me.
You know when I sit down and when I rise up;
    you discern my thoughts from far away.
You search out my path and my lying down,
    and are acquainted with all my ways.
Even before a word is on my tongue, O Lord, you know it completely.
You hem me in, behind and before, and lay your hand upon me.
Such knowledge is too wonderful for me;
    it is so high that I cannot attain it.

Where can I go from your spirit? Or where can I flee from your presence?
If I ascend to heaven, you are there;
    if I make my bed in Sheol, you are there.
If I take the wings of the morning
    and settle at the farthest limits of the sea,
even there your hand shall lead me, and your right hand shall hold me fast.

For it was you who formed my inward parts;
    you knit me together in my mother's womb.
I praise you, for I am fearfully and wonderfully made.
    Wonderful are your works; that I know very well.

Search me, O God, and know my heart; test me and know my thoughts.
See if there is any wicked way in me, and lead me in the way everlasting.

PSALM 139: 1-10, 13-14, 23-24

SESSION 3

Individual and Family of Origin

Session 3 has two purposes: (1) to help you reflect on who you are right now, and (2) to discuss the influence of your family of origin (the family from which you have come) on your marriage.

Before marriage, it is very important to explore who you are. Have you thought about your personality traits, values, and attitudes toward life? Have you considered how your strengths and weaknesses might influence the shape of your marriage? In order for marriage to be a concrete symbol of God's covenant of love, you must be aware of who you are and what you bring to marriage. Honestly looking at yourself and your background will help you to be open to Christ's presence in your life and in your relationship.

In every marriage, two people join together to form a special union. One goal of Christian marriage is for you to bring yourselves fully to the relationship and to create a unique relationship that will be greater than either individual person. Christians believe that Christ is at the center of this new creation. In order to embody Christ, you must be aware of who you are, and what you contribute to this relationship. Reflecting on yourselves in this way can help you to appreciate the depth and beauty of what you bring to a marriage in Christ.

> *One goal of Christian marriage is for you to bring yourselves fully to the relationship and to create a unique relationship that will be greater than either individual person.*

How do you reflect on yourselves? One way to begin is to look at your "personality." We like to view personality as a set of traits that can have a profound effect on the way we see life. For example, some people get their energy from inside themselves. These people may be happy with quiet time to think, plenty of space, and a good book. Some people tend to be energized by others. They may enjoy big parties, the noise and crowds of the city, and lots of excitement. While we don't want to oversimplify or stereotype, we do want you to see that people react to life in different ways. Because you are two individuals coming together to form a couple, you must be aware of your view toward life and recognize your partner's view.

While personality traits, heredity and environment affect you as people, you have the ability and the power to grow and change.

☞

Just because you have a specific outlook on life, however, does not mean that you are programmed to act in a predetermined way. You are a blend of thoughts and feelings, heredity and environment. While personality traits, heredity and environment affect you as people, you have the ability and the power to grow and change.

In other words, you have freedom of choice. In every situation, you can and do make choices. However, choice is limited. As much as you might like to, you cannot choose to fly without a vehicle!

Because we all have freedom of choice, we have responsibility for our behavior and emotions. Therefore, thinking, freedom and responsibility are tied together. Choosing freely means that we recognize the connection between our choices and their consequences. For example, suppose you choose to go to an all night party on Sunday night. You may be fine on Monday morning, or you may be so tired that you can barely function at work. Staying out all night is only a true choice if you *understand* and *accept* the consequence that other things may happen because of your behavior.

Since we have freedom to choose, we have some power to plan and control our lives. However, many things are out of our control and we waste valuable time, effort, and resources trying to

We can't change or control other people.

☞

control them. For example, we can't control the weather, the stock market and many other things that affect our lives. Some people spend so much time and effort trying to change things over which they have no control that they miss the opportunity to change the things that they can.

We can't change or control other people. People often get themselves into trouble by trying to control the behavior of others. This is not to say that you can't influence people with your words and actions; it just means you have little hope of getting them to do exactly what you want them to do all of the time. While we may be able to influence change or support our partners when they want to change, we cannot force them to do so!

Remember that people have power only if they take the time to understand what they can do, accept the responsibilities and consequences of their choices, and make the best choices that they can. An understanding of oneself, with one's strengths and weaknesses, is critical for a healthy relationship. In other words, you must enter marriage with a realistic understanding of who you are.

In addition to the things you personally bring to marriage, you also bring all sorts of things from your families of origin. While many couples think that as long as they are in love, their families do not matter, studies show that our families of origin do affect us—consciously or unconsciously. Awareness of your family background is essential for building a healthy marriage.

An understanding of oneself, with one's strengths and weaknesses, is critical for a healthy relationship.

It is important to recognize that you have learned, and will continue to learn, many things from your families. Throughout your lives, for example, you have observed in your families what it means to be a male or a female, what it means to be married, and what "permanent commitment in marriage" means. In recent years, more people have experienced divorce in their families than ever before. This certainly has had an effect on the way some couples understand the permanence of marriage. Some families taught their members about faith, and its role in married life. Were your parents religious? Did their attitudes about religion affect the way you understand faith and church? These are good questions to ask.

Growing up, you learned about many simple life activities from your families. For example, what was your family's attitude toward housework and other chores? Were some chores "female" and others "male"? Will you look at chores in the same way as your family did? What do you think about the relationship between work and family? Did your mother work outside the home? Did your parents share home responsibilities equally, or did one parent bear most of the household responsibility regardless of whether he or she worked outside the home? How will this affect your decisions and actions?

As you became an adult, you probably began to notice other things that took place in your families. For example, how did your parents relate to their in-laws? Did they get along with each other, or was there tension most of the time? How did your grandparents fit into your family? Were they people you saw on holidays, or people you saw every day? Were extended family events the center of your social life, or did you grow up seeing little of your cousins or other relatives?

Our families of origin do affect us— consciously or unconsciously.

In some families, there are issues that affect every member. A common issue is the abuse of alcohol or other chemical by one or more family members. If one of you has come from a substance abusing family, there may be repercussions that you do not even realize. Some adult children of substance abusers demonstrate strong insecurities, primarily because their home environment may have been insecure. Others may have a strong need to control every situation because they had such little control over the home environment when a substance abuser lived there. It is crucial to recognize that substance-abusing family members, particularly parents, play a significant role in shaping *our* adult lives.

In reflecting on family issues, we believe that several important questions arise: (1) Are you and your partner aware of the things from your family that affect you as an adult? (2) Do you and your partner agree on the way you will approach family of origin issues? (3) Do you like the way you were raised, or would you like to do things differently from your family or that of your partner?

As members of families, you bring experiences to your marriage. If you are aware of what you have brought from your respective families, you can use that knowledge to strengthen your marriage. If you are unaware of the traits and attitudes that influenced you, you may be destroyed by them. For better or for worse, all of us are influenced by the type of family from which we have come. These factors may affect our future relationships.

If you are aware of what you have brought from your respective families, you can use that knowledge to strengthen your marriages.

We all must address family of origin issues early on in our relationships We will not always agree on how to handle the elements of our lives that we bring from our families, but we must be aware of them and communicate effectively about them. We must also be willing to give and take about some family of origin issues. An inability to negotiate about family of origin issues can lead to serious tension in a marriage relationship.

Who Am I?

· HIS SHEET ·

On this side of the sheet, list five of your strengths and five of your weaknesses, and on the other side, five strengths and five weaknesses of your partner. Discuss your lists with each other for ten minutes—talk about how you perceive yourselves and each other.

My strengths:

    1.

    2.

    3.

    4.

    5.

My weaknesses:

    1.

    2.

    3.

    4.

    5.

Who Are You?

· **HIS SHEET** ·

My partner's strengths, as I see them:

    1.

    2.

    3.

    4.

    5.

My partner's weaknesses, as I see them:

    1.

    2.

    3.

    4.

    5.

Who Am I?

· HER SHEET ·

On this side of the sheet, list five of your strengths and five of your weaknesses, and on the other side, five strengths and five weaknesses of your partner. Discuss your lists with each other for ten minutes—talk about how you perceive yourselves and each other.

My strengths:

1.

2.

3.

4.

5.

My weaknesses:

1.

2.

3.

4.

5.

ℐↄ

Who Are You?

My partner's strengths, as I see them:

1.

2.

3.

4.

5.

My partner's weaknesses, as I see them:

1.

2.

3.

4.

5.

Group Discussion

As a group, choose two or three questions and discuss them for about 10-15 minutes. If there are individual questions that you feel are unresolved, you can continue to discuss them by yourselves or with your sponsors at another time.

1. What characteristics do we acquire from our families?

2. What did I learn about faith in God from my family?

3. What family traditions and customs will we pass on to our children? Which ones will we eliminate from our new family?

4. How much of what we learned from our families do we want to repeat in our marriages?

Notes

Self-Evaluation

· HIS SHEET ·

The purpose of this activity is to help you pinpoint the ways you feel about yourself right now. It is not a test, but a springboard for your discussion. You may not be aware of it, but your fiancée may not always know how you feel about yourself!

Directions: Remember, this is not a test. It is just a scale to help you assess where you feel you are as an individual, right now. Complete the scale by circling the number that best describes how you feel about each pair of words. Where do you stand? After you have finished your sheet, share your answers with your partner. Did you learn anything new about her?

worthless	1	2	3	4	5	worthwhile
my life is empty	1	2	3	4	5	my life is full
inadequate	1	2	3	4	5	adequate
stupid	1	2	3	4	5	smart
incompetent	1	2	3	4	5	competent
naive	1	2	3	4	5	knowledgeable
can't do anything right	1	2	3	4	5	can't do anything wrong
guilty	1	2	3	4	5	not guilty
immoral	1	2	3	4	5	moral
anxious	1	2	3	4	5	calm
unassertive	1	2	3	4	5	assertive
unattractive	1	2	3	4	5	attractive
depressed	1	2	3	4	5	happy
bad	1	2	3	4	5	good
lonely	1	2	3	4	5	not lonely
unloved	1	2	3	4	5	loved
misunderstood by others	1	2	3	4	5	understood by others
bored	1	2	3	4	5	interested

Notes

Self-Evaluation

· HER SHEET ·

The purpose of this activity is to help you pinpoint the ways you feel about yourself right now. It is not a test, but a springboard for your discussion. You may not be aware of it, but your fiancé may not always know how you feel about yourself!

Directions: Remember, this is not a test. It is just a scale to help you assess where you feel you are as an individual, right now. Complete the scale by circling the number that best describes how you feel about each pair of words. Where do you stand? After you have finished your sheet, share your answers with your partner. Did you learn anything new about him?

worthless	1	2	3	4	5	worthwhile
my life is empty	1	2	3	4	5	my life is full
inadequate	1	2	3	4	5	adequate
stupid	1	2	3	4	5	smart
incompetent	1	2	3	4	5	competent
naive	1	2	3	4	5	knowledgeable
can't do anything right	1	2	3	4	5	can't do anything wrong
guilty	1	2	3	4	5	not guilty
immoral	1	2	3	4	5	moral
anxious	1	2	3	4	5	calm
unassertive	1	2	3	4	5	assertive
unattractive	1	2	3	4	5	attractive
depressed	1	2	3	4	5	happy
bad	1	2	3	4	5	good
lonely	1	2	3	4	5	not lonely
unloved	1	2	3	4	5	loved
misunderstood by others	1	2	3	4	5	understood by others
bored	1	2	3	4	5	interested

Notes

Family Traditions Discussion

This activity is designed to help you reflect on the importance of traditions and customs in your marriage. It also should help you reflect on the ways you agree or disagree about the meaning of family traditions and how you will (or will not) incorporate them into your marriage. Take some time this week to think about these questions, and answer them using the following procedure.

- First, sit by yourselves and write out answers to the questions on your individual worksheets.
- Next, exchange your answers and read them by yourselves.
- Discuss your answers, pointing out areas of agreement and trying to resolve any disagreements.
- Try to write a joint answer to the questions.

Discussion Questions

1. If I had to choose one or two traditions, customs, or attitudes from my family of origin what would they be? How would I incorporate them into our new family?

2. Do we agree on the things we would bring to our new family? Why or why not?

His Family Traditions Worksheet

1. If I had to choose one or two traditions, customs, or attitudes from my family of origin what would they be? How would I incorporate them into our new family?

2. Do we agree on the things we would bring to our new family? Why or why not?

Family Traditions Discussion

· HER SHEET ·

 This activity is designed to help you reflect on the importance of traditions and customs in your marriage. It also should help you reflect on the ways you agree or disagree about the meaning of family traditions and how you will (or will not) incorporate them into your marriage. Take some time this week to think about these questions, and answer them using the following procedure.

- First, sit by yourselves and write out answers to the questions on your individual worksheets.
- Next, exchange your answers and read them by yourselves.
- Discuss your answers, pointing out areas of agreement and trying to resolve any disagreements.
- Try to write a joint answer to the questions.

Discussion Questions

---

1. If I had to choose one or two traditions, customs, or attitudes from my family of origin what would they be? How would I incorporate them into our new family?

2. Do we agree on the things we would bring to our new family? Why or why not?

1. If I had to choose one or two traditions, customs, or attitudes from my family of origin what would they be? How would I incorporate them into our new family?

2. Do we agree on the things we would bring to our new family? Why or why not?

Prayer for the Week

Lord, make me an instrument of your peace.
Where there is hatred, let me sow love;
where there is injury, pardon;
where there is doubt, faith;
where there is despair, hope;
where there is darkness, light; and
where there is sadness, joy.

O Divine Master, grant that I may not seek so much
to be consoled as to console;
to be understood as to understand;
to be loved as to love.

For it is in giving that we receive,
it is in pardoning that we are pardoned, and
it is in dying that we are born to eternal life.

Amen.

PRAYER OF ST. FRANCIS

SESSION 4

Values in Marriage

As adults, we often are called upon to make choices that reflect our values. Many of us have faced situations where we've had to make hard choices or decisions because our values demanded them. In marriage, our values also play an important role. For example, because you have chosen to marry in the Church, you are asserting that you are willing to accept the values of the Catholic tradition (if you are Catholic), and to respect them if you come from another religious heritage. We hope that you will get the support to live these values from each other, your families and friends, and your local church communities.

As you know, developing and nurturing your values is a lifetime project. Just as you grow and change, your values will continue to grow and develop. Furthermore, a mature conscience is something that grows with time, prayer and work. Learn to appreciate your developing Christian values and Christian conscience.

Developing and nurturing your values is a lifetime project.

Session 4 has two main purposes: (1) We will explore the various ways people develop values, and the ways that the church can support marriage. (2) We will discuss the role of conscience in Christian marriage, paying particular attention to the steps for forming a mature adult Christian conscience.

Where do you get your values? Think back to each stage of your life, and see if this sounds familiar to you. As children, you develop many of your values from your parents and other significant adults. What Mom and Dad do and say have a great impact on what you do and say. When you reach school age, you also assimilate values from your friends and teachers. Later, especially as you approached adolescence, the role of your peers becomes absolutely crucial. What your parents think matters less than what your friends think about any given topic. If you come from a religious family, your church communities may also play a major role in the development of your values. In this case, values from the Bible, Church traditions, and local faith communities may be very important to you. Certainly, the culture in which you live exerts varying degrees of influence on you everywhere you turn.

One of the hallmarks of maturity is that you can develop a value system that takes into account all . . . elements, and reflects who you are as individuals.

A

One of the hallmarks of maturity is that you can develop a value system that takes into account all of these elements, and reflects who you are as individuals. Adults accept some values from their key groups, reject others, and develop a mature value system that works for them.

Values influence your lives in many ways, including the choice of a marriage partner. You may not be aware of this, but some studies show that common values are a major predictor of marital success. We tend to look for someone whose life vision is the same as ours. We also look for someone whose strengths complement ours.

You may see some strong differences between you and your partner. However, while your personalities may be different, in a successful marriage your basic values in life will be consistent. Serious marital problems can arise if your basic life values differ greatly. For example, if one

Marriage is a permanent commitment.

A

partner believes that you choose a job simply on the basis of salary, but the other thinks that it is important to derive satisfaction from work, difficulties may arise. If one person values faith deeply, but the other person doesn't respect religious values at all, you may experience serious problems unless you can come to consensus about how you will handle your faith differences. While some differences in major values need not point to an immediate disaster—it does signal the need for serious conversation and open communication.

The Catholic Church holds some basic values about marriage. For example, we deeply believe that marriage is a permanent commitment. While we recognize that some marriages fail, we hope that whenever possible, couples can resolve their differences so that their permanent commitment of marriage will be upheld.

The Church believes openness to life is an important value in marriage.

A

The Church also believes that openness to life is an important value in marriage. This means that we are open to the possibility of having and nurturing children. Furthermore, it implies that we are open to strategies and techniques that build up our relationships, and that we work at developing ways to enhance our marriages day after day. Openness to life also assumes that we are sensitive and aware of the needs of those around us, and are willing to respond to them in a loving, giving way.

Another value that is critical to a Christian view of marriage is the importance of sharing faith in relationship. This can be a significant issue if you are of different traditions, but it also can affect the relationship if the two of you are of the same religion but do not practice it to the same extent. For many couples, sharing faith is not something that happens naturally or easily. In our work with couples, we have found that many partners are uncomfortable with the idea of sharing faith with each other, even if they belong to the same church. Our advice to you is to talk about your faith sometime before you get married, and try to decide how you will share it on a regular basis. We recommend that you try praying with each other. This may be uncomfortable for some couples, but we have found that it gets much easier as you pray together on a regular basis.

What happens if your religious traditions are different? Is it possible to truly share faith in two-church environment? Many couples of different traditions share their faith on a daily basis. We have found that the answer to these questions is yes: they start sharing faith by looking for the things they have in common. For two Christians, belief in

Values help you clarify who you are.

Jesus Christ and the covenant of marriage will form a basis for shared faith. Bible reading and prayers such as the Lord's prayer will be common in all Christian traditions. Christians and Jews share a belief in one God and a common vision that the Hebrew Bible is God's Word. Praying together with the psalms, reflecting on the meaning of the prophets or other readings from the Hebrew Bible can provide the basis for shared prayer and reflection. Persons who are married to adherents to other religions may find their common faith in things such as nature and the wonders of the world. Common prayer may simply include acknowledging the presence of a supreme being who has given us the universe.

Values help you clarify who you are. What you hold as valuable shapes you not only as an individual, but affects your relationship as well. In a Christian marriage, the values of the Church community play a crucial role for couples. Church communities have a responsibility to support couples as they try to live their values of faith and marriage.

Furthermore you are called to put your values into action—to be honest, to be life-giving, to have integrity, not to look the other way in the face of evil or unethical behavior. We believe that we are challenged to follow our consciences in setting life's goals and making life's decisions. What does conscience mean? According to the *Catechism of the Catholic Church,* no.1778, conscience is: "a human person recognizing and acting on the moral quality of concrete actions." In other words, conscience means

You are called to put your values into action—to be honest, to be life-giving, to have integrity.

that you weigh your decisions based on a number of important factors such as reflection and prayer, the teaching of the Bible and the Church, and the advice of others. Following your conscience is particularly significant whenever you are involved in a decision of consequence, particularly when there are costs and benefits from a number of choices.

Developing conscience in marriage means that you will work to become aware of what it takes to do the right thing in easy and difficult situations. In Catholic tradition, there is a discernment process that helps you come to conclusions about issues. Discernment simply means the ability to figure out whether something is right or wrong, or good or bad for us. First, you must pray for God's guidance. Being open to God's will lays the groundwork for any further discernment. Second, you must gather information about the issue, just as you would gather information before you purchase a house or a car or something else of significance. Third, it is often helpful to consult with someone whose wisdom and advice you trust. Getting an objective opinion about an issue can provide clarity and help facilitate your decision. Fourth, evaluate your conclusions throughout the process. Also, be open to reevaluation after you have made your decision—you may find other factors that change your decision.

In Catholic tradition, conscience formation plays an important role in adult moral development. Carefully formed consciences provide us with the moral framework to live as adult believers. Sharing the discernment process in marriage is a rewarding and demanding element of the faithful relationship.

Should a situation arise where you as a couple conclude that you disagree in conscience with the Church's official teaching on a subject, your *formed* conscience must be your guide, according to Catholic tradition. However, saying that your conscience has been "formed" assumes that you have done everything in your power to follow the discernment process outlined above. Reflection and discernment must come before any conclusion is reached.

Developing conscience in marriage means that you will work to become aware of what it takes to do the right thing in easy and difficult situations.

When you begin your marriage, you will pledge to enter into a covenant relationship with each other. You will promise to be "sacraments" or symbols of Christ's love to each other and the world. As you live your marriage relationship, you will grow in your ability to be symbols of Christ. You can teach each other and support each other as you struggle with conscience issues in all areas of life.

Marriage Mission Statement: Our Values

· COUPLE SHEET ·

Many companies and other organizations such as parishes have recently developed mission statements. These are usually two- to four-paragraph statements which try to sum up what the company or organization believes and how it tries to act. For this activity, each couple should take about fifteen minutes to develop an outline for a marriage mission statement. Use these questions as a guide:

1. **What do you want your marriage to say to the world?**

2. **What couple actions best sum up your relationship?**

When you have finished, share your mission statement with your sponsor couple, and then take it home and work on it during the week!

Notes

Couple Discussion on Values

· HIS SHEET ·

Remember how important it is to *form* a Christian conscience for the best possible outcome of any decision you and your partner must make. Carefully review the formation process.

Steps for Forming Christian Conscience

1. Open yourselves to the will of God through prayer. Discerning God's will in your lives is a crucial step in forming conscience.

2. Gather as much information as possible about the situation involved. This includes finding out what the Bible says and what the Church teaches on an issue, and involves evaluating the beliefs and principles that we have retained from our families, friends, education, and other sources.

3. Consult someone who can provide objectivity and insights.

4. If this is a decision that affects both parties in the relationship, make sure that the values of both parties are taken into account.

5. Be willing to re-evaluate the original decision if it doesn't seem to be right, or if conditions change.

Directions:
Take five minutes to write down your top five values in life. Then compare and discuss your lists with your partner.

His Values Worksheet

My five top values in life are:

1.

2.

3.

4.

5.

Couple Discussion on Values

· HER SHEET ·

Remember how important it is to *form* a Christian conscience for the best possible outcome of any decision you and your partner must make. Carefully review the formation process.

Steps for Forming Christian Conscience

1. Open yourselves to the will of God through prayer. Discerning God's will in your lives is a crucial tep in forming conscience.

2. Gather as much information as possible about the situation involved. This includes finding out what the Bible says and what the Church teaches on an issue, and involves evaluating the beliefs and principles that we have retained from our families, friends, education, and other sources.

3. Consult someone who can provide objectivity and insights.

4. If this is a decision that affects both parties in the relationship, make sure that the values of both parties are taken into account.

5. Be willing to re-evaluate the original decision if it doesn't seem to be right, or if conditions change.

Directions:
Take five minutes to write down your top five values in life. Then compare and discuss your lists with your partner.

Her Values Worksheet

My five top values in life are:

1.

2.

3.

4.

5.

My Priorities

· HIS SHEET ·

 The purpose of this activity is to help you clarify and articulate your priorities, both individually and as a couple. In marriage, it is important to know where your priorities are and also to know where you stand in relationship to your spouse's priorities. Take some time this week to think about this exercise, and use the following procedure.

Directions: Separate and fill out your Priorities worksheets, placing your choices in rank order (1 is your first choice and 5 is your last choice). Add or subtract your own priorities. Use the other side of the sheet to explore what's important to you. Come together and discuss your answers. Complete a third sheet together. Have you achieved consensus?

Money priorities	Time priorities
Buying a new car	Spending time with my spouse
Buying a house	Spending time with my friends
Spending money on clothes	Spending time with my family of origin
Spending money on education	Pursuing hobbies
Spending money on vacations	Working

My Priorities

· HER SHEET ·

 The purpose of this activity is to help you clarify and articulate your priorities, both individually and as a couple. In marriage, it is important to know where your priorities are and also to know where you stand in relationship to your spouse's priorities. Take some time this week to think about this exercise, and use the following procedure.

Directions: Separate and fill out your Priorities worksheets, placing your choices in rank order (1 is your first choice and 5 is your last choice.) Add or subtract your own priorities. Use the other side of the sheet to explore what's important to you. Come together and discuss your answers. Complete a third sheet together. Have you achieved consensus?

Money priorities	Time priorities
Buying a new car	Spending time with my spouse
Buying a house	Spending time with my friends
Spending money on clothes	Spending time with my family of origin
Spending money on education	Pursuing hobbies
Spending money on vacations	Working

Her Priorities Worksheet

Our Priorities

The purpose of this activity is to help you clarify and articulate your priorities, both individually and as a couple. In marriage, it is important to know where you stand with your priorities, and also to know where you stand in relationship to your spouse. Take some time this week to think about this exercise, and use the following procedure.

Directions: Based upon your individual worksheets and being sure to include other considerations that are important to you, rank your priorities on a scale of 1 to 5 (first to last choice). Have you achieved consensus?

Money priorities	Time priorities
Buying a new car	Spending time with each other
Buying a house	Spending time with our friends
Spending money on clothes	Spending time with our families of origin
Spending money on education	Pursuing hobbies
Spending money on vacations	Working

Couple Priorities Worksheet

Prayer for the Week

And God said: "Let the earth bring forth living creatures of every kind: cattle and creeping things, and wild animals of the earth of every kind." And it was so. God made the wild animals of the earth of every kind, and the cattle of every kind, and everything that creeps upon the ground of every kind. And God saw that it was good.

Then God said: "Let us make humankind in our image, according to our likeness; and let them have dominion over the fish of the sea, and over the birds of the air, and over the cattle, and over all the wild animals of the earth, and over every creeping thing that creeps upon the earth."

So God created humankind in his image,
in the image of God he created them;
male and female he created them.

God blessed them, and God said to them, "Be fruitful and multiply, and fill the earth and subdue it; and have dominion over the fish of the sea, and over the birds of the air, and over every living thing that moves upon the earth." And it was so. God saw everything that he had made, and indeed, it was very good.

GENESIS 1: 24-28, 29b-31

SESSION 5

Intimacy and Sexuality

Session 5 has two basic purposes: (1) to discuss the centrality of intimacy and sexuality in our lives, and (2) to introduce the Church's teaching on intimacy and sexuality.

Intimacy and sexuality are central elements of any marriage. Developing an intimate relationship is at the heart of our understanding of married life, because it is in becoming close, in sharing deeply, in trusting and respecting one another, that we can come to understand the depth of God. Intimacy in marriage can take many forms. Much of intimacy is linked with communicating our deepest selves, so good communication and intimacy go hand in hand. Developing intimacy, like developing other aspects of your lives, takes place over many years.

In marriage, a critical area of intimacy is sexual intimacy. It is important to emphasize that everything you do is influenced by your sexuality—by the simple fact that you are male or female, and by the fact that you bring to this relationship various attitudes about sex. Sexuality is *who* you are—and sexual activity is a way to express your sexuality.

It is important to remember that intimacy is not simply something you "do" in marriage; it is at the heart of all relationships. Being intimate with another person implies a willingness to know your partner and to let yourself be known. Openness is central to the idea of an intimate relationship. It would be very difficult to think that a relationship is open if two people do not know each other very well.

Intimacy also presumes trust and friendship. An intimate relationship is one where two people trust each other enough to communicate effectively with each other, listen

Developing an intimate relationship is at the heart of our understanding of married life.

Intimacy is linked with communicating our deepest selves.

to each other, and be there for each other. These are just a few elements of intimacy that are crucial to this discussion.

Intimacy is at the heart of all relationships.

Another factor to remember is that achieving intimacy does not happen overnight. As with any other aspect of relationship, building intimacy takes considerable time and effort. This is why it is so strange to hear people talk about "being intimate" with each other when they do not even know each other! In most cases, building intimacy is a developmental process that grows as the relationship grows.

A crucial element of intimacy in marriage is commitment. Knowing that the other person is there for you unconditionally allows great freedom for an individual. If you are confident of your partner's love and commitment, the crises of life will not destroy you. Confidence in and intimacy with each other can help sustain you through good times and bad.

Recognizing the need for intimacy has always been a part of the Judeo–Christian tradition. In Genesis, chapter 2, the author tells us that it is not good for the man to be alone—therefore an equal partner is made for him. As a church community, we believe that intimacy involves equality of the partners, not domination of one over the other. Furthermore, marriage is never an excuse to abuse your partner sexually. As we have already stated, any type of domestic violence stands in opposition to the way the Church understands marriage in Christ.

A crucial element of intimacy in marriage is commitment.

One important element of marital intimacy is sexual expression. Recent Catholic teaching on marriage clearly states that marriage is *incarnational*—it develops in and through, not apart from, our bodies. Church teaching on sexuality, therefore, emphasizes positive attitudes about the body and sexual expression. Catholic tradition on intimacy emphasizes the connections among marriage, sexual expression, permanent commitment, love, and life.

Many people are unaware or misinformed about current Roman Catholic teaching on sexuality. While it is certainly true that throughout much of our history, the Church saw sex as something to be tolerated, and not as a wonderful gift from God, this is not the case today. Early in the church's history, the celibate life was seen as the higher calling, while marriage was thought of as a lesser calling. People believed this for a variety of reasons. Some theologians stressed that marriage was a distraction, while celibacy allowed the Christian to devote himself or herself to God. Others emphasized the idea that sex was less than holy, because it was lustful, or simply because it was too physical to

Intimacy involves equality of the partners.

be holy. Up until the Second Vatican Council, which took place in the 1960's, the Church taught that the primary purpose of sexual intercourse was procreation.

As a result of the Second Vatican Council, the Church's official teaching on sexuality and sexual intercourse evolved. In the document entitled "The Pastoral Constitution on the Church in the Modern World," the Church highlighted the idea that marriage is a holy way of life, and that sexual intercourse in marriage is a gift from God.

Marriage is incarnational—it develops in and through, and not apart from, our bodies.

*C*atholic teaching on sexuality and sex since the Second Vatican Council can be summed up in these fundamental beliefs:

1. We are all created sexual beings by God. Therefore, sexuality is a gift from God.

2. Sexual intercourse is one of the most complete gifts that one person can give to another. Therefore, it requires a permanent commitment. Many secular and religious studies show why this is true. For example, some studies indicate that couples who live together before marriage are less likely to marry each other. One reason might be that they are unable to make a permanent commitment. For the Church community, commitment and sexual gift - giving go together!

3. We believe that every occasion of sexual intercourse has two equal purposes—the love and support of the couple, and the possibility of new life. The Second Vatican Council changed past Church teaching which said that procreation was the main purpose of sexual inter- course. However, it also stated that love and life can not be separated.

4. In the past, the Church taught that sexual intercourse was primarily for procreation. Any other reason was secondary. Today, the Church recognizes our sexual natures and activities as being gifts from God. Like any other gift, however, it has the potential to be abused. The Church believes strongly that sexual intercourse should be part of a committed marriage, and should be life-giving to both parties.

5. Because love and life cannot be separated, the Church teaches that every act of sexual inter- course must be open to the possibility of life. Therefore, the only legitimate form of birth regulation is Natural Family Planning (NFP). The reason for this is that couples using con- traception are separating the two purposes of intercourse by blocking a pregnancy while still engaging in intercourse. With NFP, couples prevent pregnancy by choosing not to en- gage in intercourse.

Every occasion of sexual intercourse has two equal purposes— the love and support of the couple, and the possibility of new life.

Natural Family Planning (NFP) is a method of birth regulation that relies on the careful monitoring of a woman's monthly menstrual cycle. By avoiding sexual intercourse during ovulation and the time around ovulation, it is possible to avoid pregnancy. Ovulation (when an egg is released from the ovaries) occurs ten to sixteen days before the beginning of a menstrual period, and is the time when a woman can conceive a child. On the other hand, planning intercourse during the time of ovulation can result in a greater likelihood of pregnancy, if that is the desired outcome.

NFP is not like calendar rhythm, which relies on an average of past cycles to determine when couples need to abstain from sexual intercourse. Calendar rhythm does not provide an accurate way to monitor monthly variations in cycle length, and is therefore ineffective.

In order to be successful in using the method, you must take classes, but the basic components of fertility awareness as taught in NFP are as follows:.

- When a woman gets close to ovulation, her basal body temperature rises slightly, (by tenths of degrees.) To determine when the temperature rise begins, it is necessary for a woman to take her temperature each day, before she gets out of bed, and record the temperature.

- As a woman gets close to ovulation, the secretions from her vagina change. They become wet and develop the consistency of egg whites to protect the sperm and help nourish it.

- As a woman approaches ovulation, the cervical *os* (the mouth of the womb) opens to accept sperm.

- Around the time of ovulation, some women experience individual indicators such as cramps, mood swings, breast tenderness, and changes in sexual desire.

- Reliability of NFP depends on careful charting and interpretation of these fertility signs, and a joint commitment to abstinence during the times of fertility (usually five to seven days per month).

- The Church supports birth regulation using Natural Family Planning because it does not interfere with the inseparable connection between the two purposes of sexual intercourse: the love of the spouses and openness to the possibility of new life.

For further information on NFP, consult your Diocesan Office of Family Ministry.

Sexual intimacy is one concrete way to express the total commitment you make to each other in marriage. Building intimacy is vital to marriage because it helps you to share more deeply about all aspects of life. Throughout your lives, intimacy will enhance the quality of your relationship.

The Church recognizes our sexual natures and activity as being gifts from God.

Beliefs and Ideas about Intimacy and Sexuality

· HIS SHEET ·

For the following beliefs and ideas about sex, check whether you think the statement is true or false. Use page 80 to elaborate on these statements and the questions that follow.

Statement	True	False
Sex is natural.		
Humans have no control over their sexual impulses.		
Sex is only for procreation.		
Sex is a source of pleasure.		
Men want sex more than women.		
Sex and intimacy are the same thing.		
I feel very comfortable talking about sex and sexuality.		
My parents spoke openly to me about sex.		
My future spouse and I have had discussions about sex.		
Attractiveness is a crucial aspect of good sexuality.		
Good sexual functioning requires only a knowledge of the biology of sex.		
The most important sexual organ is the brain.		
Modesty and shame are not the same thing.		
It is important that couples have premarital sex in order to insure compatibility.		
Sexual compatibility is built on relationship compatibility.		
Any sexual thought is a sin.		
Love and sex are two different things.		
Extramarital affairs can sometimes be good for a marriage.		
It is not possible to have the same excitement about sex throughout your whole marriage.		
Wives need to learn to tolerate sex for their husband's sake.		

Couple Discussion on Intimacy and Sexuality

· HIS SHEET ·

Choose one or two questions from each of the following groups and write the answers on your worksheet. Share the answers with your partner. Take no more than ten minutes.

Discussion Questions

Group A:

1. How have we experienced intimacy?
2. Are there areas of our relationship where we have not begun to achieve intimacy?
3. Can we change those things?

Group B:

1. How willing am I to discuss my sexual attitudes and values with my partner?
2. Am I afraid of sharing my attitudes and values about sex?
3. How will communicating about sex affect our relationship?

Beliefs and Ideas about Intimacy and Sexuality

· HER SHEET ·

For the following beliefs and ideas about sex, check whether you think the statement is true or false. Use page 82 to elaborate on these statements and the questions that follow.

Statement	True	False
Sex is natural.		
Humans have no control over their sexual impulses.		
Sex is only for procreation.		
Sex is a source of pleasure.		
Men want sex more than women.		
Sex and intimacy are the same thing.		
I feel very comfortable talking about sex and sexuality.		
My parents spoke openly to me about sex.		
My future spouse and I have had discussions about sex.		
Attractiveness is a crucial aspect of good sexuality.		
Good sexual functioning requires only a knowledge of the biology of sex.		
The most important sexual organ is the brain.		
Modesty and shame are not the same thing.		
It is important that couples have premarital sex in order to insure compatibility.		
Sexual compatibility is built on relationship compatibility.		
Any sexual thought is a sin.		
Love and sex are two different things.		
Extramarital affairs can sometimes be good for a marriage.		
It is not possible to have the same excitement about sex throughout your whole marriage.		
Wives need to learn to tolerate sex for their husband's sake.		

◢

Couple Discussion on Intimacy and Sexuality

· HER SHEET ·

◢ Choose one or two questions from each of the following groups and write the answers on your worksheet. Share the answers with your partner. Take no more than ten minutes.

Discussion Questions

Group A:

1. How have we experienced intimacy?
2. Are there areas of our relationship where we have not begun to achieve intimacy?
3. Can we change those things?

Group B:

1. How willing am I to discuss my sexual attitudes and values with my partner?
2. Am I afraid of sharing my attitudes and values about sex?
3. How will communicating about sex affect our relationship?

ACTIVITIES FOR THE WEEK

The Bull's Eye—A Model for Intimacy

· HIS SHEET ·

The purpose of this activity is to explore the levels of intimacy that we share with a variety of people. Psychologists tell us that our life experiences are like a bull's eye. On the outside rim are the things that you share easily and with many people. As you move toward the center, there are things in your lives that you share with very few people, or no one. Marriage is one of the most intimate relationships we have. In marriage, two bull's eyes overlap to one degree or another. How much do your bull's eyes overlap? How willing are you to be intimate with your fiancée? Take some time this week to think about this activity, and use the following procedure.

1. Write down one thing for each level of the bull's eye. Use the attached sheet. What things are easy to share with others? What things are difficult or impossible to share with others?

2. During the week, share your bull's eye with your partner. Were you surprised? Did it reinforce your understanding of your partner?

3. Complete another sheet for your relationship. Where can you grow in intimacy?

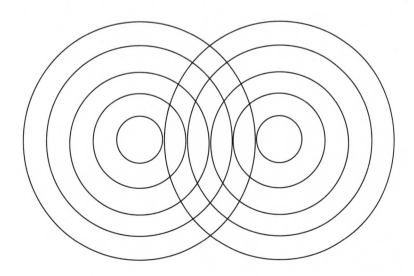

His Bull's Eye Worksheet

Level 1: Something about myself that I would share with anyone.

Level 2: Something about myself that I would share with people I see every day.

Level 3: Something about myself that I would share with family members and friends.

Level 4: Something about myself that I would only share with my best friend.

Level 5: Something about myself that I would share only with my spouse.

Level 6: Something about myself that I would not usually share with anyone.

The Bull's Eye—A Model for Intimacy

· HER SHEET ·

The purpose of this activity is to explore the levels of intimacy that we share with a variety of people. Psychologists tell us that our life experiences are like a bull's eye. On the outside rim are the things that you share easily and with many people. As you move toward the center, there are things in your lives that you share with very few people, or no one. Marriage is one of the most intimate relationships we have. In marriage, two bull's eyes overlap to one degree or another. How much do your bull's eyes overlap? How willing are you to be intimate with your fiancé? Take some time this week to think about this activity, and use the following procedure.

1. Write down one thing for each level of the bull's eye. Use the attached sheet. What things are easy to share with others? What things are difficult or impossible to share with others?

2. During the week, share your bull's eye with your partner. Were you surprised? Did it reinforce your understanding of your partner?

3. Complete another sheet for your relationship. Where can you grow in intimacy?

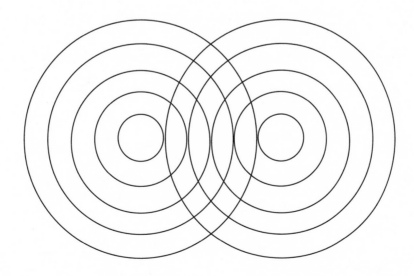

Her Bull's Eye Worksheet

Level 1: Something about myself that I would share with anyone.

Level 2: Something about myself that I would share with people I see every day.

Level 3: Something about myself that I would share with family members and friends.

Level 4: Something about myself that I would only share with my best friend.

Level 5: Something about myself that I would share only with my spouse.

Level 6: Something about myself that I would not usually share with anyone.

The Bull's Eye—A Model for Intimacy

· COUPLE SHEET ·

❧ Draw the two bull's eyes, with as many levels as you like. Overlap them as they represent the level of intimacy in your relationship. Explore the ways you reveal yourselves to each other on your Couple Worksheet. Discuss with each other how you can risk becoming more intimate.

Couple Bull's Eye Worksheet

Level 1: Something about myself that I would share with anyone.

Level 2: Something about myself that I would share with people I see every day.

Level 3: Something about myself that I would share with family members and friends.

Level 4: Something about myself that I would only share with my best friend.

Level 5: Something about myself that I would share only with my spouse.

Level 6: Something about myself that I would not usually share with anyone.

$\mathcal{L}\!\!\!\!\mathcal{D}$

Couple Discussion on the
Catholic Church's Thinking on Sexuality

· HIS SHEET ·

$\mathcal{L}\!\!\!\!\mathcal{D}$ The purpose of this exercise is to help you clarify your understanding of the Church's teaching on sexuality. How will you respond to it? Take some time this week to think about these questions, and use the following procedure.

Directions: Sit by yourselves and write out answers to the questions. Exchange your answers and read them by yourselves. Then discuss your answers, pointing out areas of agreement and trying to resolve any disagreements.

Discussion Questions

1. How do I understand the Church's teaching on sexuality?

2. How will this teaching on sexuality affect our married life?

Notes

✍

Couple Discussion on the
Catholic Church's Thinking on Sexuality

✍ The purpose of this exercise is to help you clarify your understanding of the Church's teaching on sexuality. How will you respond to it? Take some time this week to think about these questions, and use the following procedure.

Directions: Sit by yourselves and write out answers to the questions. Exchange your answers and read them by yourselves. Then discuss your answers, pointing out areas of agreement and trying to resolve any disagreements.

Discussion Questions

1. How do I understand the Church's teaching on sexuality?

2. How will this teaching on sexuality affect our married life?

Notes

Prayer for the Week

For this reason I bow my knees before the Father, from whom every family in heaven and on earth takes its name. I pray that, according to the riches of his glory, he may grant that you may be strengthened in your inner being with power through his Spirit, and that Christ may dwell in your hearts through faith, as you are being rooted and grounded in love. I pray that you may have the power to comprehend, with all the saints, what is the breadth and length and height and depth, and to know the love of Christ that surpasses knowledge, so that you may be filled with all the fullness of God.

EPHESIANS 3: 14-19

SESSION 6

⌒

Balancing Practical Issues in Relationship

In any relationship, the day-to-day aspects of life some-times receive little attention. However, practical issues such as household management, finance, juggling careers and family are of great concern to newly married couples. In our fast-paced, high-pressure society, couples often are pulled away from each other by a variety of concerns. For example, studies show that financial pressures on many couples are great, and young couples struggle to attain things that their parents took for granted. Furthermore, gender roles from previous generations are not clearly defined now, adding to the stress for newly married couples.

For a couple beginning a marriage in faith, daily issues also include a religious dimension. For example, are your life's priorities consistent with your faith or in conflict with it? How do your decisions about issues such as the meaning of work, the meaning of money, or the way you spend time stack up against the values you discussed in Session 4?

While no single session will get at all the practical issues that you will face, we hope to help you surface some issues that are important to you. Many of you have already dealt with some of these issues, but it never hurts to bring them front and center once again. Here are some ex-amples of issues you might face: (1) How do you decide who assumes household tasks (especially the distasteful ones?) (2) How do you make financial decisions? (3) How do you decide how and with whom to spend your time? (4) How do you evaluate the role of faith in your lives?

In discussing any of these practical issues, you can use the skills you learned in *Unitas*. For example, you can use your communication skills to determine interests, likes,

Are your life's priorities consistent with your faith or in conflict with it?

⌒

[An] issue for many newly married couples is trying to create a balance between work and home.

⌒

dislikes and expectations. You can use your awareness of personality traits and expectations to determine suitability for tasks. For example, if one of you likes to handle money and happens to be good in math—that person can oversee balancing checkbooks and other financial details. You can use your ability to make informed values decisions to resolve major issues.

Use your awareness of personality traits and expectations to determine suitability for tasks.

One important issue for many newly married couples (and for many couples at all stages in married life!) is trying to create a balance between work and home. Sharing your insights, experiences, and expectations on this topic can be very helpful for everyone. As you probably have experienced, there are several ways that you can look at the relationship between marriage and work. In some families, for example, one partner will be the sole wage earner and the other will work primarily at creating and maintaining a home. This arrangement assumes that one partner can support the family, and that the other partner is willing to work in the home. Of course, in our society, many people can continue to work from a home office, allowing considerable flexibility for spouses.

Some couples have a "dual job" arrangement. This means that both partners work outside the home to one extent or another. It does not mean, however, that both partners have equal commitments to their jobs. One might be in a career, while the other may simply be trying to earn a little extra money to make ends meet. In this situation, one person's job may take priority over the other.

A "dual career" family means that both partners' work involves a considerable investment of time and effort, and that their jobs will be more than simply a means to make money. In general, "dual career" couples have invested a considerable amount of time, effort, and money to build their careers. The office may be a very important center of life for each person.

Gender expectations often color decisions about careers and jobs.

While couples must ask questions about the ways that they balance work and family, the issues sometimes are magnified in the two-career household. For example, how do dual career couples find adequate time to build their marriage relationships? How often do they see each other? In the future, what happens when children are born? What arrangements must be made to maintain the two-career lifestyle, or what sacrifices must be made to enable one parent to spend more time with children? These and other important questions frequently are in the minds of the two-career couple.

You should also be aware that gender expectations often color decisions about careers and jobs. Together, you must explore the ways that your expectations of what men and women do affect the way you balance work and family. Whose career takes priority? Is this defined by gender? Are earning power and decision-making linked? Is this defined by gender? You must address these and other questions like them as you navigate the complex waters of work and family.

There is no one right answer to questions raised.

In this area, as in so many others, there is no one right answer to questions raised. You must answer them in light of your goals and values, your expectations and life objectives. We hope that this session raises some issues for you, and helps affirm the decisions you have already made. A nice thing to remember is that even though formal marriage formation will end soon, you can take with you the tools you've learned here to continue your discussions of these and other practical issues.

IN-SESSION COUPLE ACTIVITIES

Beliefs and Ideas about Marriage Priorities

· HIS SHEET ·

For the following beliefs and ideas about marriage priorities, check whether you think the statement is true or false.

Statement	True	False
It is necessary for couples to have a mutually agreed upon budget.		
I am clear about how my future spouse defines the word "necessity."		
My future spouse thoroughly understands my current financial obligations.		
My future spouse and I agree on the use of credit cards.		
My future spouse and I have discussed and agreed on a savings plan for our future.		
My future spouse and I agree on the way we will make charitable contributions.		
I know and have shared with my future spouse which household chores I like to do and the ones I don't like to do.		
My future spouse and I are comfortable with our behavioral styles (neatness, personal grooming, etc.).		
My future spouse and I have discussed how we like to spend our leisure time.		
I believe that buying a house is the first priority for a married couple.		
I want to wait some time before we have our first child.		
I think we should spend most holidays with my parents.		
My future spouse and I like each others' friends.		
I think it is important for each spouse to have social engagements with friends alone.		
My future spouse and I plan to spend a lot of time with our families.		
My future spouse and I have discussed the faith issues in our relationship.		
My future spouse and I have planned our wedding ceremony.		
My future spouse and I have discussed how we'll raise our children in terms of religion.		
My future spouse and I share the same commitment to faith.		

Beliefs and Ideas about Work and Career

· HIS SHEET ·

For the following beliefs and ideas about work and career, check whether you think the statement is true or false.

Statement	True	False
My career takes priority over everything else.		
My future spouse and I both value each others' careers.		
If my spouse were offered a job in a different city, I would quit my job and go.		
Wives should only have part-time jobs or no job at all.		
A wife can have a job as long as she is able to get all of the household chores completed.		
A husband should take a personal day from work if his wife needs him to do things so she can go to work.		
A man's responsibility to his family comes before his responsibility to his career.		
A job is only important to get the money to do the things we want to do.		
Everyone needs to have meaningful work to feel good about themselves.		
Career decisions are family decisions.		
I would support my spouse if he or she wanted to quit work and go back to school.		
A parent's education has a higher priority than a child's education.		
One parent should be with a child all day long even if it means someone has to quit his or her job.		
A wife should quit her job if a parent needs her to take care of him or her.		

Beliefs and Ideas about Marriage Priorities

· HER SHEET ·

For the following beliefs and ideas about marriage priorities, check whether you think the statement is true or false.

Statement	True	False
It is necessary for couples to have a mutually agreed upon budget.		
I am clear about how my future spouse defines the word "necessity."		
My future spouse thoroughly understands my current financial obligations.		
My future spouse and I agree on the use of credit cards.		
My future spouse and I have discussed and agreed on a savings plan for our future.		
My future spouse and I agree on the way we will make charitable contributions.		
I know and have shared with my future spouse which household chores I like to do and the ones I don't like to do.		
My future spouse and I are comfortable with our behavioral styles (neatness, personal grooming, etc.).		
My future spouse and I have discussed how we like to spend our leisure time.		
I believe that buying a house is the first priority for a married couple.		
I want to wait some time before we have our first child.		
I think we should spend most holidays with my parents.		
My future spouse and I like each others' friends.		
I think it is important for each spouse to have social engagements with friends alone.		
My future spouse and I plan to spend a lot of time with our families.		
My future spouse and I have discussed the faith issues in our relationship.		
My future spouse and I have planned our wedding ceremony.		
My future spouse and I have discussed how we'll raise our children in terms of religion.		
My future spouse and I share the same commitment to faith.		

Beliefs and Ideas about Work and Career

· HER SHEET ·

 For the following beliefs and ideas about work and career, check whether you think the statement is true or false.

Statement	True	False
My career takes priority over everything else.		
My future spouse and I both value each others' career.		
If my spouse were offered a job in a different city, I would quit my job and go.		
Wives should only have part-time jobs or no job at all.		
A wife can have a job as long as she is able to get all of the household chores completed.		
A husband should take a personal day from work if his wife needs him to do things so she can go to work.		
A man's responsibility to his family comes before his responsibility to his career.		
A job is only important to get the money to do the things we want to do.		
Everyone needs to have meaningful work to feel good about themselves.		
Career decisions are family decisions.		
I would support my spouse if he or she wanted to quit work and go back to school.		
A parent's education has a higher priority than a child's education.		
One parent should be with a child all day long even if it means someone has to quit his or her job.		
A wife should quit her job if a parent needs her to take care of him or her.		

FOCCUS Follow-Up: Balancing Practical Issues

· COUPLE WORKSHEET ·

The purpose of this activity is to help focus your attention on issues that may arise early in your marriage. While some of these questions may seem very simple, answering them can present some surprising (and sometimes disturbing) results. Recall the results of your FOCCUS inventory. Do you have unresolved issues around some of these questions? Try discussing those first. Take some time this week to think about the questions, and use the following procedure.

- First, sit by yourselves and write out answers to two of the questions on your worksheet. Choose the questions that are most important to you.
- Next, exchange your answers and read them by yourselves.
- Discuss your answers, pointing out areas of agreement and trying to resolve any disagreements
- Try to write a joint answer to the questions.

Discussion Questions

1. What are our financial priorities?

2. How will we set up and maintain our household?

3. How will we balance other relationships in the first year of marriage?

4. How will we integrate faith into our daily lives?

5. How will we balance career and family?

Couple Practical Issues Worksheet

His Practical Issues Worksheet

1. What are our financial priorities?

2. How will we set up and maintain our household?

3. How will we balance other relationships in the first year of marriage?

4. How will we integrate faith into our daily lives?

5. How will we balance career and family?

Notes

Her Practical Issues Worksheet

1. What are our financial priorities?

2. How will we set up and maintain our household?

3. How will we balance other relationships in the first year of marriage?

4. How will we integrate faith into our daily lives?

5. How will we balance career and family?

Notes

Prayer for the Week
ℐ𝒶

*L*et love be genuine; hate what is evil, hold fast to what is good; love one another with mutual affection; outdo one another in showing honor. Do not lag in zeal, be ardent in spirit, serve the Lord. Rejoice in hope, be patient in suffering, persevere in prayer. Contribute to the needs of the saints; extend hospitality to strangers.

Bless those who persecute you; bless and do not curse them. Rejoice with those who rejoice, weep with those who weep. Live in harmony with one another; do not be haughty, but associate with the lowly; do not claim to be wiser than you are. Never repay anyone evil for evil, but take thought for what is noble in the sight of all. If it is possible, so far as it depends on you, live peaceably with all.

ROMANS 12: 9-18

SESSION 7

Developing a Spirituality of Marriage

Session 7 has two main purposes: (1) to discuss the idea that spirituality is connected to every part of your life and (2) to explore the ways that you can build faith in your homes.

We believe that developing a spiritual life is a concrete way of acting on your faith. For example, when you consider the role of God in the day-to-day events of life, you develop a sense of spirituality. When you ask the question "What would Jesus do in this situation?" you can begin to see that faith and ordinary life are intimately connected.

When you ask the question "What would Jesus do in this situation?" you can begin to see that faith and ordinary life are intimately connected.

We think it is easy to see how marriage gives you many opportunities to be spiritual people. Our spirituality is not simply defined by the number of hours we spend in church, but by the way we experience God in and through our spouses, our children, and our extended families and friends. A shared spirituality is a solid foundation on which to rest your entire relationship.

We strongly believe that leading a spiritual life can be closely linked with the concepts and skills you've been working on in *Unitas*. For example, we think that spirituality is linked to an awareness that you are created in God's image and likeness. Furthermore, it is influenced by your ability to communicate, to share values, and to relate intimately with each other. We hope you will recognize that growth in spirituality is a process that takes a lifetime. We encourage you to explore your spirituality now, and to think about the possibilities for growth in your spiritual life.

We experience God in and through our spouses, our children, and our extended families and friends.

An important starting point for shared spirituality is the idea of marriage as a covenant relationship.

Building a shared spiritual life does not require that you share the same religious tradition. As we have stated many times throughout the sessions, we recognize and respect the diversity of faith present in the Church and interfaith couples. We also have considered the many ways that you can share a spiritual life regardless of the similarities or differences in your religious traditions. For example, no matter what your religion is, you can be aware of God working in and through your spouse. Together, you can experience God in other people, you can share prayer and other expressions of faith, and you can learn about each other's traditions. More than anything else, you can support each other and help each other to grow in your own faith traditions. Even if your religions are different, you can help each other to live as children of God.

In our experience, we have found that an important starting point for any couple's shared spirituality is the idea of marriage as a covenant relationship. As you may remember, a covenant marriage binds us through unconditional love—like God's love for us. The Catholic perspective on marriage is that it is a sacrament—in other words, marriage calls us to embody God's unconditional love, the covenant, through our daily actions. You as couples are living, breathing expressions of God's unconditional love. While no one can live this love perfectly, we try each day to grow as symbols of God's covenant with us. Regardless of your religious tradition, you can accomplish this goal through ordinary life events and people—through your relationships with families and friends, by the way you conduct yourselves in the workplace, and by the way you relate to each other.

Catholics also believe that marriage is a vocation in the Church (from the Latin, *vocare*, which means "to call"). When you say "yes" to the sacrament of marriage, you commit each day to love each other as Christ loves you. A Sacramental marriage is not something that simply happens on the wedding day, it is something that you *live* every day. Through the vocation of Christian marriage, you will have daily opportunities to build faith in your hearts and homes. However, building faith in your families doesn't mean that you spend all your time on your knees. It simply means that you take special care to find Christ in all you do and in all the people you meet, and that you work to build faith through the ordinary events of your lives.

When you say "yes" to the sacrament of marriage, you commit each day to love each other as Christ loves you.

The idea that you can build faith in your homes is a strong part of recent Catholic tradition. Many church leaders have written about the idea that the Christian family finds numerous ways to build faith in the home. One of the strongest advocates of this concept is Pope John Paul II. In his 1981 letter *Familiaris Consortio*, he discusses four ways that Christian families can be centers of faith. While others could certainly be included, these tasks communicate the essence of what it means to build faith in our homes.

According to Pope John Paul, faith-filled families first must form a community of persons. In other words, before you can reach out to others, you must work to build your own relationship. Many church documents emphasize the fact that couples should build a partnership that is based on love and life. Building a community of persons assumes that you trust each other and have respect for

Families first must form a community of persons.

each other. It presupposes that you communicate effectively with each other. Forming a community of persons means that you see each other as equals, no matter what roles you assume in the relationship. It means that you protect the vulnerable in your homes, especially the very young and the very old.

Next, families can be centers of faith by serving life. This can take many forms. An obvious way for couples to serve life is to have children and educate them, but this certainly is not the limit of service to life. Families are called upon to teach each other that all life is sacred, to share that respect for life with others, and to make sacrifices so that life is protected. They promote life by welcoming children into their families through birth or adoption. For some couples, it might mean welcoming a child into their homes through foster care or being a "parent" to children in the community. For some people, serving life will mean taking a stand on issues such as assisted suicide, abortion, unemployment, immigration, housing and a host of others. Above all, serving life means that you model behavior that

Families are called upon to teach each other that all life is sacred, to share that respect for life with others, and to make sacrifices so that life is protected.

supports the Church's view that says all life is sacred whether a person is rich or poor, young or old, educated or uneducated.

Third, families can be centers of faith by building up society. As families, you are called to reach beyond your selves to help make the world a better place. You will have many opportunities to do so. For example, you can teach each other civic responsibility by emphasizing the importance of involvement in the community. You can foster care for the environment by being aware of the way you treat the earth and its products. These are just a few ways that you can participate in the development of society as a whole.

Finally, families can be centers of faith by sharing in the mission and life of the Church. It is important for you to remember that you *are* the church. However, you are not church in isolation. We are all part of local communities, and part of the universal Church. Therefore, we share in the mission of the Church on many levels. In your homes, you share in the mission of

You are *the church, part of local communities and part of the universal Church.*

the church daily. Through the ordinary events of your lives, you help make Christ present. For example, when you are there for someone who needs you, you share in the Church's mission. When you share a family meal, give thanks, and take time to recall who we are, you "celebrate" the Eucharist in your homes. When you forgive and are forgiven, the ministry of reconciliation becomes a part of your family life. These are just some examples—there are many more. Each day of your lives, you can share in the mission of the Church by recognizing that the faith of the Church can be found in the things you do day after day.

Building faith in your homes is a way of life. It takes commitment, time and effort, and it grows over time. It doesn't happen magically on a wedding day, but takes a life of working together. We strongly believe that building faith in our families is a way to grow in our spirituality. Even though it presents challenges, it is well worth the effort required.

IN-SESSION ACTIVITIES

What Helps Me to Develop My Spirituality?

· HIS SHEET ·

Please separate for about five minutes. Think about the items on this list. Choose five items that can help you develop as a spiritual person. Share these items with your fiancée and your sponsor couple, and discuss what things you have in common, and what differences you have. How can you grow in spirituality as a couple?

Item	Yes	No
Hiking in the woods		
Playing with children		
Quietly reading a book		
Talking with your partner		
Praying		
Going to the store for your partner		
Visiting your family		
Going to Mass or other church services		
Making love		
Voting		
Mowing the lawn for a neighbor		
Reading the Bible		
Recycling your garbage		
Working at a soup kitchen		
Donating money to a charity		
Painting your mother's kitchen		
Sharing an afternoon at the beach with your partner		

Building Spirituality as a Couple

Separate for about five minutes to think about the last few weeks of your life. List five things that you have done as a couple to build your spirituality. Have you as a couple reached out to another person? Have you prayed with each other? Share these things with each other and with your sponsor couple.

1.

2.

3.

4.

5.

IN-SESSION ACTIVITIES

What Helps Me to Develop My Spirituality?

· HER SHEET ·

Please separate for about five minutes. Think about the items on this list. Choose five items that can help you develop as a spiritual person. Share these items with your fiancée and your sponsor couple, and discuss what things you have in common, and what differences you have. How can you grow in spirituality as a couple?

Item	Yes	No
Hiking in the woods		
Playing with children		
Quietly reading a book		
Talking with your partner		
Praying		
Going to the store for your partner		
Visiting your family		
Going to Mass or other church services		
Making love		
Voting		
Mowing the lawn for a neighbor		
Reading the Bible		
Recycling your garbage		
Working at a soup kitchen		
Donating money to a charity		
Painting your mother's kitchen		
Sharing an afternoon at the beach with your partner		

Building Spirituality as a Couple

Separate for about five minutes to think about the last few weeks of your life. List five things that you have done as a couple to build your spirituality. Have you as a couple reached out to another person? Have you prayed with each other? Share these things with each other and with your sponsor couple.

1.

2.

3.

4.

5.

Concluding Session Prayer

Leader: In the name of the Father, and of the Son, and of the Holy Spirit. **All:** Amen.

Leader: Let us pray: Life-giving God, we thank you for your gifts, especially the gift of these engaged and married couples. Help them to grow in faith and love for each other and You. Be with them today and throughout their married lives. We make this prayer through Christ our Lord. Amen.

Scripture Reading: John 15: 9-12

As the Father has loved me, so I have loved you; abide in my love. If you keep my commandments, you will abide in my love, just as I have kept my Father's commandments and abide in his love. I have said these things to you so that my joy may be in you and that your joy may be complete. This is my commandment, that you love one another as I have loved you.

Leader: The Gospel of the Lord.   **Response:** Praise to you, Lord Jesus Christ.

Intercessions: The response to our prayers is: **God of life, hear our prayer.**

- For the church, which stands as a light of hope in the midst of the world, we pray:
- For the world, which needs strong witnesses of love, we pray:
- For the poor and powerless in our midst, that God will provide for them, we pray:
- For all married couples, especially those who are struggling, we pray:
- For our families and friends, that we may live in peace with them, we pray:
- For all couples preparing for marriage, that they may grow in love and commitment, we pray:
- For any prayers that you would like to share: (pause) we pray:

Final Reflection: Participants can take a few minutes to share their reflections on *Unitas*.

Leader: Let us conclude our prayer today by joining hands and praying in the words that Jesus gave us. Our Father...

Final Blessing:
May God bless us and keep us.
May God's face shine upon us.
May God look upon us kindly and give us peace.
Amen.

Giftedness

· HIS SHEET ·

This activity is designed to help you see the relationship between what you do at home and what you can do in the community of the church. Watch for parallels! Take some time this week to think about this exercise, and use the following procedure.

1. Divide the "Notes" page in half.

2. On one side of the page, write down five things that you do very well.

3. On the other side, write down the ways that your gifts can be shared with your family and your local church community.

4. Discuss your answers with your partner.

5. Make a plan with your partner to share one of your talents with your family and your local church community.

Notes

Giftedness

· HER SHEET ·

This activity is designed to help you see the relationship between what you do at home and what you can do in the community of the church. Watch for parallels! Take some time this week to think about this exercise, and use the following procedure.

1. Divide the "Notes" page in half.

2. On one side of the page, write down five things that you do very well.

3. On the other side, write down the ways that your gifts can be shared with your family and your local church community.

4. Discuss your answers with your partner.

5. Make a plan with your partner to share one of your talents with your family and your local church community.

Notes

UNITAS EVALUATION

· HIS SHEET ·

✍ Please complete this evaluation and hand it to your team leaders at the end of the last session.

The purpose of this evaluation is to get your feedback on the *Unitas* sessions that you just completed. Your input will help us to improve the process for the future. Thank you for your time and effort.

Directions: Please CHECK the response that best describes your experiences overall in these sessions and answer the questions on page 126. Please write any additional comments regarding specific sessions in the space provided.

Question	Not at all	A little	Somewhat	Very much
1. How comfortable was the parish space?				
2. Were the married couples prepared with all the materials they needed for the sessions?				
3. Did the married couples begin and end the session on time?				
4. Did you have a break in the middle of the sessions?				
5. Did the married couples understand and communicate the material that they were supposed to present?				
6. Were the married couples able to answer your questions?				
7. Was the content of the sessions presented at the proper level for you?				
8. Did the married couples explain the topic at the beginning of each session?				
9. Did you feel that your opinions were important to the conversation?				
10. Were the couple activities held during the sessions helpful to you?				

Unitas Comments and Suggestions

· HIS SHEET ·
---

1. Which session or sessions did you find most helpful?

2. Why?

3. Which session or sessions did you find least helpful?

4. Why?

5. What comments or suggestions do you have that might help improve the process?

UNITAS EVALUATION

· HER SHEET ·

✍ Please complete this evaluation and hand it to your team leaders at the end of the last session.

The purpose of this evaluation is to get your feedback on the *Unitas* sessions that you just completed. Your input will help us to improve the process for the future. Thank you for your time and effort.

Directions: Please CHECK the response that best describes your experiences overall in these sessions and answer the questions on page 126. Please write any additional comments regarding specific sessions in the space provided.

Question much	Not at all	A little	Somewhat	Very
1. How comfortable was the parish space?				
2. Were the married couples prepared with all the materials they needed for the sessions?				
3. Did the married couples begin and end the session on time?				
4. Did you have a break in the middle of the sessions?				
5. Did the married couples understand and communicate the material that they were supposed to present?				
6. Were the married couples able to answer your questions?				
7. Was the content of the sessions presented at the proper level for you?				
8. Did the married couples explain the topic at the beginning of each session?				
9. Did you feel that your opinions were important to the conversation?				
10. Were the couple activities held during the sessions helpful to you?				

Unitas **Comments and Suggestions**

· HER SHEET ·

1. Which session or sessions did you find most helpful?

2. Why?

3. Which session or sessions did you find least helpful?

4. Why?

5. What comments or suggestions do you have that might help improve the process?

Notes

Notes

Notes

Notes